Smile'z

A cleft adventure from birth to nine
written by a boy born with cleft.

Author: Quin Zahniser

Copyright © 2022 by Quin Zahniser

All rights reserved. No parts of this publication may be reproduced or transmitted in any form or by any means, mechanical or electronic to include photocopying and recording, without the prior written consent of the publisher, except in the case of brief quotations embodied in literary reviews.

Hi, My name is Quin, my dad calls me Smile^Z.

Even though we look different, we should all be treated the same.

I have two brothers "Zman", he's two years older than me and "A", he's my identical twin without cleft.

I was born with a severe unilateral cleft lip and palate. Sometimes it is hard to make friends because people think I am ugly, but I think I am cool just because of the way I look. My dad taught me to face my differences and say, "I was born with my nose just like you were born with yours."

I hope you enjoy my book.

Your Champ,

Smile^z

A cleft is a separation or split
in either the upper lip or the
roof of the mouth (palate)
or sometimes both. It occurs
when separate areas of the
face do not join together
properly when a baby is
developing in the

Before I was born my mom and dad went to the children's hospital to learn more about my cleft.

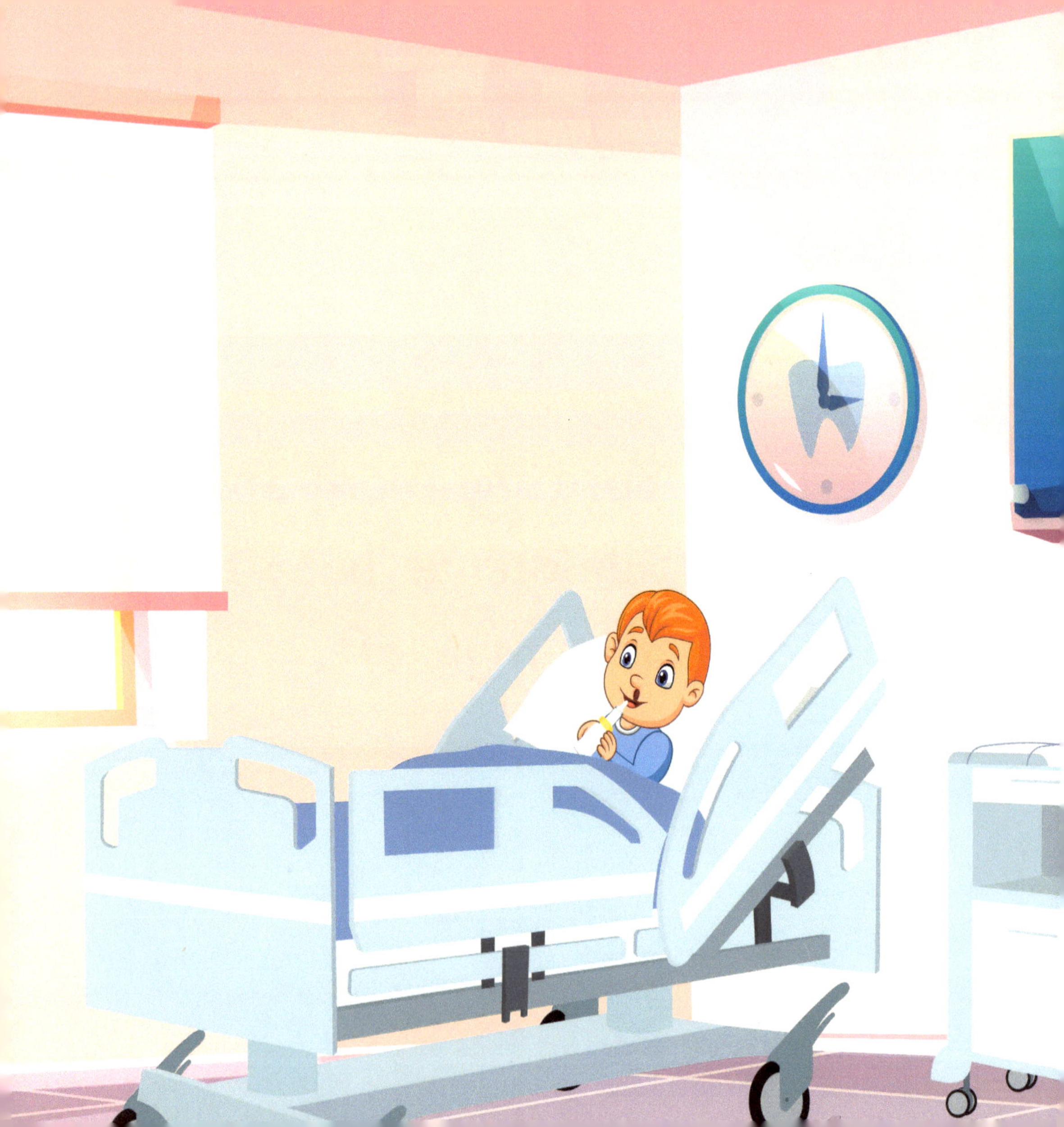

When I was born the hospital had special bottles to help me eat.

A week after I was born, the doctors at the Children's Hospital made a plan to make me look like a champ.

They told my Mom and Dad that they will make changes to the plan as I grow, because it depends on how fast I grow.

My first step to looking this good was my NAM (nasoalveolar molding). That is just a fancy name for a retainer.

At eight months old I had surgery to repair my *lip* and nose.

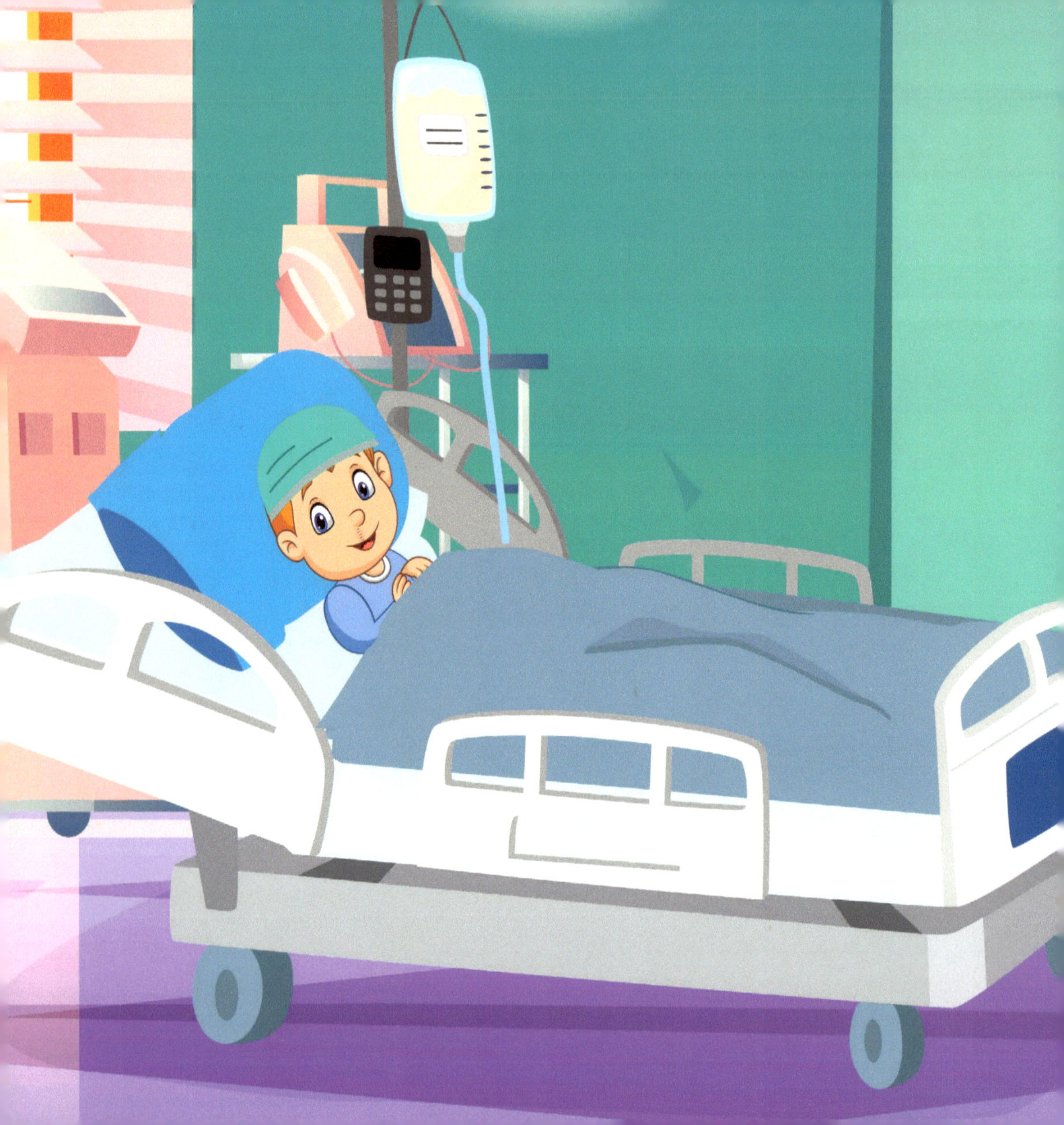

When I came out of surgery I was acting differently, but when the medicine wore-off I was normal again.

I had splints on my arms so I would not scratch my stitches.

When I turned one I had surgery to fix my palate.

This helped me eat without choking and make stronger sounds.

Before surgery I got to design my own oxygen mask with stickers and strawberry artificial food flavoring.

This helped me fall asleep thinking of strawberries.

At two I went to a speech and occupational therapist every week for the next three years.

She helped me learn to speak and play.

At six I got braces.

My parents made sure that I had a cleft experienced orthodontist.

My braces don't hurt and everyone at school likes them.

12
11
1
10
2
9
3
8
4
7
6
5
Checku
NOSE ANATOMY
TONSILS

Every year I visit my team of doctors to check on my growth and update my plan.

When I was eight I asked the doctor, "When are you going to fix my nose again? It is crooked and people tease me." He said I could come in on the next surgery day.

I was SO EXCITED!

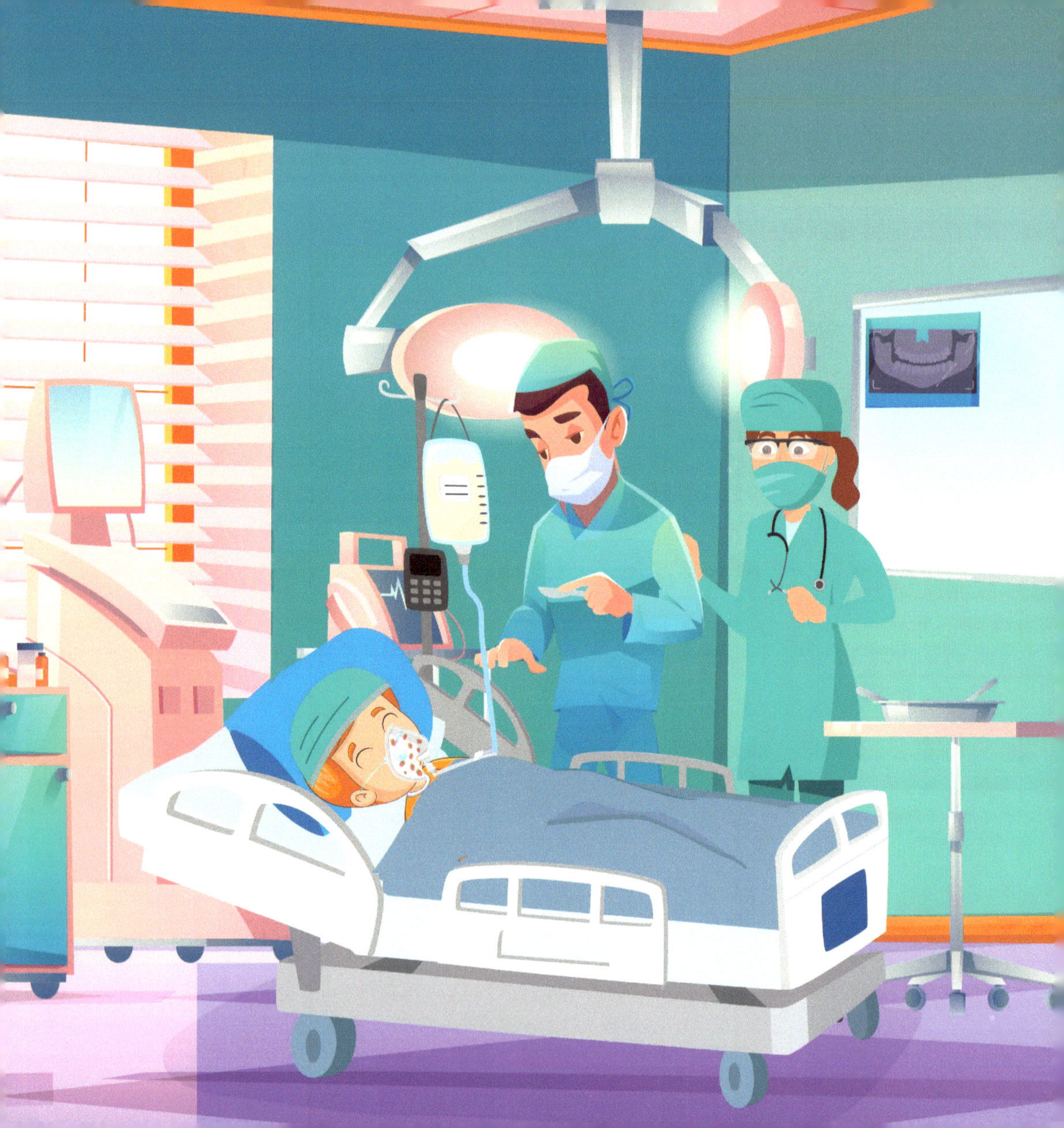

At nine I had surgery for a bone graft in my gum line.

The bone graft helped my teeth have something to grow into and make my nose and mouth straight.

I was excited to design my own oxygen mask again with the strawberry flavoring and to see what I looked like when I woke up!

We each have our own unique story. The first nine years of my life was an adventure. I am excited to hear about your adventure too at @notch.above.

CPSIA information can be obtained
at www.ICGtesting.com
Printed in the USA
BVHW021231070322
630815BV00002B/27